D0609261

text
Deborah Keenan

design concept
Larry Soule

photos
UPI: pp. 6, 10, 24, 42
Globe: pp. 14, 18, 30, 34

published by
Creative Education,
Mankato, Minnesota

Published by Creative Educational Society, Inc.,
123 South Broad Street, Mankato, Minnesota 56001
Copyright ® 1976 by Creative Educational Society, Inc. International
copyrights reserved in all countries.
No part of this book may be reproduced in any form without written
permission from the publisher. Printed in the United States.

Library of Congress Numbers: 75-39984   ISBN: 0-87191-485-9

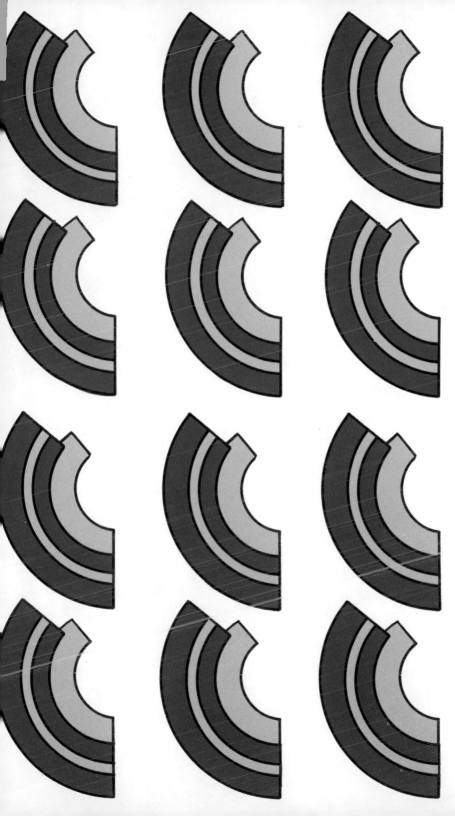

interview

Her hair is long, blonde, slightly frizzed; her body is relaxed in the chair. Her hands are as expressive as ever, though the fingernails are shorter. Her face looks beautiful to some viewers, just plain odd to others. Barbra Streisand is giving her first television interview in twelve years and people all over the country are listening and watching, trying to find out who Barbra Streisand, superstar, really is.

Today Show hostess Barbara Walters asks Streisand to explain why she hates interviews. Barbra says she is afraid of being misunderstood. She explains that appearing on T.V. is all right because, "T.V. shows you as you are." But words in a written interview don't capture the tones in a person's voice. She feels she has been mistreated by the Press. "I am amused and upset by the things I see written about me . . . they hurt me." The fear of being misunderstood, misinterpreted, and misread seems to be a basic part of Streisand's personality.

Barbara Walters asks her if she is difficult and temperamental while working. "I am not difficult to work with," Streisand states emphatically. But she also says that some people resent her wanting to do things for herself and they

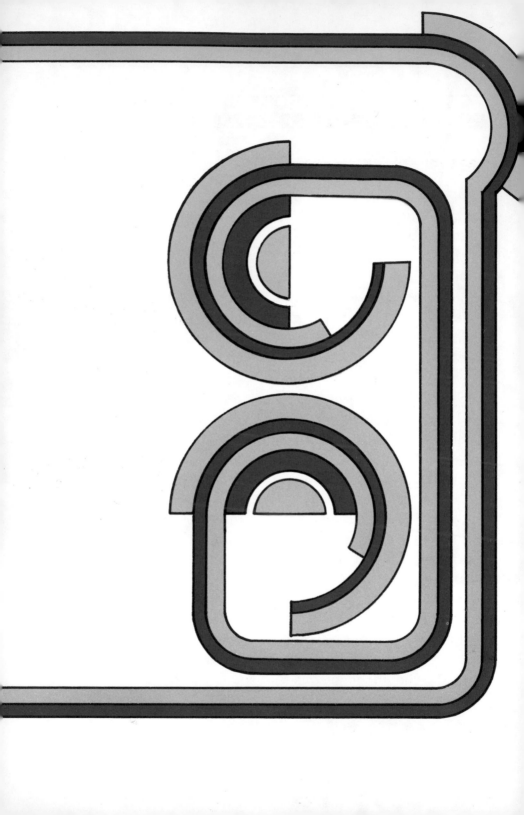

resent her being so sure she knows what is "right" for her.

During the filming of her first two musicals, **Funny Girl** and **Hello Dolly**, rumors went around that she was impossible to work with and that she tried to take over the role of director. Streisand says, "I am open to exploration. . . . I think I am fair and giving to other actors." She attributes some of her bad write-ups to the fact that she is a powerful woman in a "man's world." She explains that on a set male actors can get away with prima donna behavior, but Hollywood can't handle a woman who has opinions **and** the power to make things happen her way.

Streisand seems settled into the interview. She looks easy and relaxed and answers all the questions thoughtfully. Barbra says she is afraid of the press and of interviews, but she also knows how to use interviews to create a certain image of herself. Looking at photographs of Streisand through the years, it is easy to think of her as wearing a series of masks that hide her from people. Every new interview with her claims to be dealing with the "real" woman behind the costumes and make-up and hair-styles, but after each interview Barbra still manages to let it be known that the words on the page didn't really explain her at all. Who is Barbra Streisand?

the story

Her story is the stuff that all fairy tales are made of. Little Barbara Joan Streisand, a plain, lonely child living in Brooklyn, has grown up to become Barbra Streisand, Superstar. Barbara was born on April 24, 1942, in Brooklyn, New York. Diana and Emanuel Streisand already had a son, Sheldon, who was eight years older than Barbara. From all reports, they were a happy, close family.

Then, suddenly the stability and security of Barbara's life disappeared. Emanuel Streisand, a professor of English and Psychology, died from a cerebral hemorrhage when Barbara was fifteen months old. Mrs. Streisand, frightened and lonely after her husband's death, went to work as a bookkeeper. It was hard to raise her two children alone. Barbra says, "We were poor, but not poor poor. We just never had anything." In Barbra's mind, the loss of her father played a big part in making her what she is today. She claims, "When a child grows up missing one parent, there's a big gap that has to be filled. It's like someone being blind, they hear better. With me, I felt more, sensed more, I wanted more . . ."

Barbara grew up lonely. She was plain, and other children taunted and teased her. As Barbra

11

said later, after achieving success, "I was kind of a loner, a real ugly kid, the kind who looks ridiculous with a ribbon in her hair. And skinny. My mother wouldn't let me take dancing lessons because she was afraid my bones would break." Barbra's sense of humor and ability to laugh at herself have always helped her deal with her insecurities and fears. They have also helped her disguise her real feelings and cover any hurt she might feel.

As she grew older she retreated into fantasy worlds. She pretended to be the characters she saw in the movies or read about in books. Barbara would practice for hours in front of the mirror in order to perfect a character seen in a movie or on T.V. Her habit, which she continues today, of buying her clothes at Thrift Shops, began then because she needed costumes for the characters she created. Her choice of wardrobes also reflected her attitude about her place in life. She knew she was different from others and she made the decision to capitalize on her "kookiness" and force people to notice her.

Barbara's decision to become an actress came from those early years of feeling different from other kids, from her assuming of other personalities. Thousands of young people make that decision every day but for most it is a dreamwish, never followed up with hard work and determination. Barbara was different. Her goal was to become the most famous actress in the world and she set out to achieve that. Suddenly the play-acting in front of the mirror and the buying of weird outfits at second-hand shops wasn't a game anymore; it was a serious rehearsal for breaking into the show business world.

Barbara's unusual behavior and clothes styles created a wide gulf between her and her classmates at high school. Although Streisand got high marks, school was never a place where she felt she belonged. She never tried out for high school plays because, she remembers thinking, "Why go out for an amateurish high school production when you can do the real thing?"

When Streisand finished her sophomore year, she auditioned for a summer stock company. She was accepted and had a happy summer, but when she returned to Brooklyn she had to make some decisions about the future. Barbara's mother had remarried and Barbara's relationship with her stepfather seems to have been an unhappy one from the start. When asked about him, after achieving her success, her only response was, "He disliked me."

Her mother tried to discourage her from becoming an actress, telling her she would be hurt: "I didn't think she was pretty enough. There was no security." But everything her mother said only made Barbara more deter-

mined. When her mother suggested she'd be happier as a secretary, Barbara grew her nails several inches, "so I couldn't learn to type!"

Barbara graduated from high school in 1959 and left home. She rented an apartment in New York City and shared it with a girlfriend. When apartment sharing didn't work out, Barbara carried a cot around, sleeping in friends' apartments, studios, any place she could find. She took a job sweeping floors at the Cherry Lane Theater and met Mrs. Alan Miller, the wife of a noted acting coach. Miller agreed to coach her if she would babysit for his son. Both Miller and Eli Rill, another coach, told Barbara to work on developing her comic acting talents, but Barbara told them she wanted to be a dramatic actress.

Rill and Miller soon, however, told her the time had come when she had to start auditioning for parts in the theater. They realized that even if she didn't want to follow their advice and work on her comic talents, she had to get out and compete against other actresses in order to find out what the theater world was like.

Barbara was turned down everywhere. Most of the people she saw told her to change her nose, or her accent, or her name. Barbara would have none of it. "My kookiness," she says, "was a big, defensive, rebellious thing. But at the same time, it was theatrically right for me. I knew it." The only thing she changed was the spelling of her first name. She refused to do more than drop the "a" from Barbara because, "I wanted all the people I knew when I was younger to know it was me when I became a star."

The turning point in Streisand's professional life came in the spring of 1961. She decided to enter a talent contest. First prize was fifty dollars and also a singing engagement for a week at the Lion nightclub. She asked friends to listen to her practice her song. As she sang to them she faced the wall, unable to look into their faces while she performed. When she finished, she turned around and saw that her singing had made her friends cry.

For the contest, Barbra sang the song, "A Sleepin' Bee," which she recorded on her first Columbia album, and she won easily. It was at the Lion where Barbra started building her repertoire of strange songs and began impressing people with her unique interpretations of lyrics.

Suddenly people were rushing to see and hear Barbra Streisand as she was, dressed in thrift shop clothes, wearing outrageous make-up, acting out each song lyric as if it were an entire play. She was hired at the nightclub, Bon Soir, and was a huge success there. She appeared on local T.V. She was signed by a young talent agent. Barbra was pleased with her success as a singer but she still wanted to be a star on Broadway. "I'm not a singer. I'm an actress who sings." She went to one more audition for an off-Broadway revue, **Another Evening with Harry Stoones**. She got the part and her career as an "actress who sings" began.

career

In **Another Evening with Harry Stoones,** Barbra only had two songs to sing and she got rave reviews. Unfortunately, the play closed after one night. She went on to sing at a nightclub, The Blue Angel. Broadway producer David Merrick saw her there and signed her for the role of Miss Marmelstein, the plain, unloved secretary in the new Broadway play, **I Can Get It For You Wholesale**. The show opened in 1962 and Barbra received dazzling reviews.

In the playbill for the show Barbra had the theater writers explain in her biographical sketch that she was born in Madagascar and reared in Rangoon. As Barbra explained, "The audience would read it before I came on and notice me more." It wouldn't have mattered what was written about her. She was discovered and reviewed by the critics as the great new comedienne of Broadway.

Before the play had even opened, Barbra and the leading man, Elliot Gould, were in love. Gould has said, "I thought she was the weirdo of all times," but, "the more I got to know her, the more fascinated I was with her. She needed to be protected. She's a very fragile little girl . . . I found her absolutely exquisite." Within a year of their meeting, Streisand and Gould were married.

The play closed in December of 1962, but Streisand won the award from the New York Drama Critics for best supporting actress in a musical. After the show closed, Barbra was in demand. She appeared coast-to-coast in nightclubs and on variety shows on television. She recorded two albums for Columbia records that demonstrate her unerring sense of lyric meaning and phrasing. She took the trouble (and still does) to find the kinds of songs that were right for her. She made classic recordings of popular tunes like "Happy Days Are Here Again," and "Cry Me A River," completely changing the feeling of the songs with her interpretations.

When Streisand returned to New York in 1963 it was announced she had gotten the "plum" role for the Broadway season of 1964. She would be playing the part of Fanny Brice in the new musical, **Funny girl**.

Funny Girl tells the story of a funny Jewish girl, Fanny Brice, who was a star for years in vaudeville, on Broadway, and on radio. The producer of the show, Ray Stark, Fanny's son-in-law, decided that Barbra, another Jewish lady with a fine comic sense, should play the lead.

The play progressed, and as scene after scene was rewritten or dropped, it became apparent that the entire musical would either succeed or fail because of Barbra. She had most of the songs, most of the dialogue, was rarely off-stage. The whole show came to rest on Streisand's shoulders.

She was equal to the challenge. The show opened on Broadway on March 26, 1964. The evening, according to the critics, was one of the most memorable and exciting in Broadway history. Barbra was magnificent, and the critics almost unanimously praised her. Whitney Bolton, a New York critic wrote, ". . . Barbra Streisand . . . is talent, total, complete, utter and practicing. Vast talent, the kind that comes once in many years. That talent in **Funny Girl** flares and shimmers."

Barbra dazzled and enthralled every audience that came to the theater. She received standing ovations almost nightly, and after her rendition of the ballad, "His Is The Only Music That Makes Me Dance," anyone could look around the theater and see tears running down the cheeks of both men and women.

Barbra left the play after two years, in December of 1965. At the end of the play's run Barbra made the comment that eight performances a week on Broadway was "painful; not boring, painful! It's everything I hated about school. It's become nine-to-five." Shortly before she left the play, she had begun to make her own excitement by waiting until the last minute to

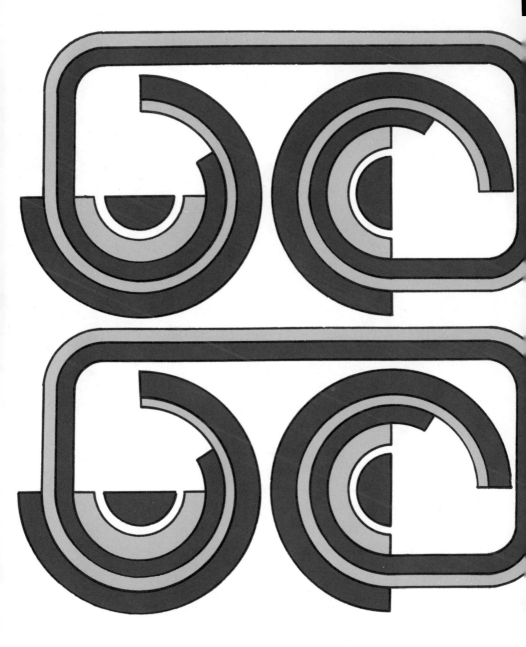

hire a taxi to take her to the theater. Sometimes there were occasions when she couldn't find a taxi. Once she flagged down a police car and had the policemen drop her at the theater; another time she asked a truck driver for a lift. As Barbra put it, "What am I going through all this agony for? All the other stars drive up in cars, and I get out of a truck."

Barbra and Elliot went to London where she performed again for a limited time in **Funny Girl**. Two months after the show opened in London, Barbra and Elliot announced the coming of their first baby. Barbra withdrew from the show and **Funny Girl** closed immediately. "This pregnancy is like a God-given thing," Barbra once told an interviewer, "and the timing couldn't be better. I was beginning to feel like a slave to my schedule. Pretty soon I'll have nothing to do but cook and be pregnant for five whole months. I can't wait!" Streisand's pregnancy seemed to calm her, and those months were the first time since leaving home at sixteen that she had ever taken time off just to rest and live an ordinary life. Jason Emanuel was born December 29, 1966. Since the London closing of **Funny Girl**, Barbra has had countless offers to return to Broadway but she has not appeared in a live musical since 1966.

24

Barbra Streisand **had** succeeded on Broadway, consequently her popularity increased enormously. She had previously been loved and adored by a small dedicated cult, but with her larger fame she managed to attract even more people willing to fight for her, praise her, deify her. Every dress she wore, every hairstyle, every fashion choice she made was followed slavishly.

The Streisand "look" was everywhere. Women struggled to grow their nails long. After seeing **Funny Girl** they asked their hairdressers to give them straight hair that curved at the shoulders in a "Streisand page-boy." When Barbra's first T.V. special was shown, women cut off their hair in order to mirror Streisand's sleek, short cut. Women spent more money than ever on eye make-up, buying bright exotic colors, and girls with large noses breathed sighs of relief when they heard that Streisand's large, irregular, Jewish nose was thought beautiful by movie critics and fans.

Barbra was worshipped by many young women because she was the supposedly plain, unwanted waif who made it big. She inspired many young people by showing them they didn't have to change themselves in order to succeed.

Doubtlessly, her place in the spotlight, though flattering, became a pressure for Streisand. She must have known that she would never be able to be alone again when she saw that so many people wanted to watch or hear everything she did or said — every gesture, every outfit she chose, every opinion she stated.

Perhaps this kind of pressure explains her response today when interviewers ask her why she hasn't done any "live" concert tours. Barbra says that she would do concerts, but personal appearances are frightening for her. As the star, she is so vulnerable to fans getting to her. She says, "I am human. I don't want to be treated not human." Barbra gives the impression that she's tired of being a symbol, a superstar; what she wants today is to do her work well and then be left alone to pursue her own interests and to be with the people she loves.

During the time that **Funny Girl** was running on Broadway and in London, Streisand recorded four more record albums and performed in T.V. specials that increased her fame, fortune, and popularity. Her albums and singles won her Grammy Awards, and her T.V. appearances won her Emmies.

Barbra's first two specials, **My Name Is Barbra** and **Color Me Barbra** were breakthroughs for television specials. In both hour-long shows Barbra was the **entire** cast. With her talent and with thousands of dollars spent on sets and costumes, Barbra filled the screen with myriad characters. Her interpretations ranged from a five year old girl, to a seventeenth century lady dancing the minuet, to a clown at the circus singing a song to an aardvark. Barbra appeared before a vast American audience, once a year for several years, and most of her specials were critically acclaimed. After signing a contract with CBS in which she promised to star in one special each year for ten years Barbra moved on to conquer another field.

Barbra left for Hollywood in 1967, with her son, to begin filming the movie version of **Funny Girl**. When Streisand landed in Los Angeles she said, "Being a star is being a **movie** star." There was no doubt that she would be as big a success in film as she had already proven to be on Broadway, on records, and on television. After the first few weeks of filming, however, rumors began to float around Hollywood that Streisand was temperamental, and that she was trying to produce and direct the movie as well as star in it.

After a few negative reports, Barbra's director, William Wyler, came to her defense and said, "Barbra is very interesting to work with. Not easy and not difficult. She is completely wrapped up in her work. She's got ideas on how to perform. Some are good, some are not good. Ten times I would rather have someone like her.

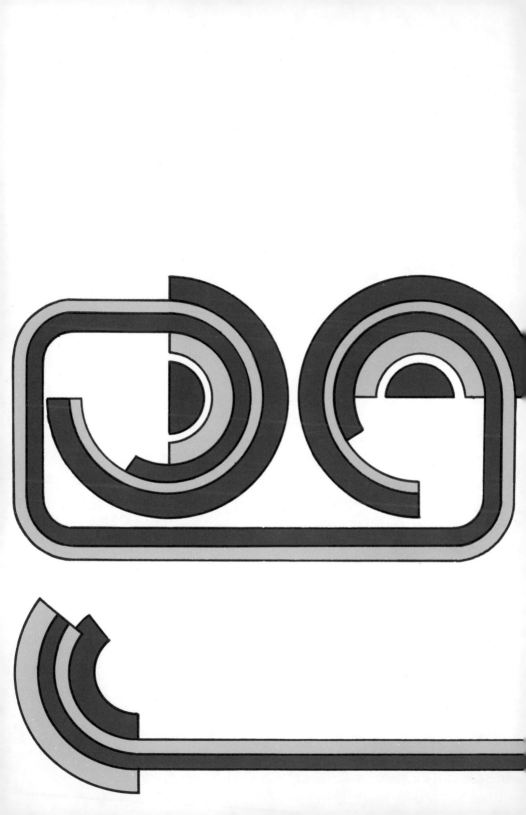

An actor has got to use his head as well as his body."

This comment helped to ease the tension on the set, but cast and crew members still let it be known that they found the "new star" pushy and a troublemaker. Rumors also started about Barbra's relationship with her leading man, Omar Shariff. Elliot Gould released a statement saying, "I love her and trust her all the way."

Whenever Elliot was interviewed, he was asked how he thought their marriage could survive. While in London with Barbra, he told a reporter, "To say I love Barbra, that's obvious. Otherwise I wouldn't have stood it. I know the traps. I know the wounds and I've decided it's worth it ... we really love each other." When the love rumors died down, the columnists finally began mentioning that scenes from the movie, already completed, were beautiful and that Streisand was wonderful in the part.

Interrupting the filming of **Funny Girl**, Streisand flew to New York in June of 1967 to do a live concert in Central Park. Over 135,000 people came to the free concert (still the largest number of people to go to any concert to see a single performer) and Barbra was an overwhelming success. The concert was filmed and later shown on television. After this appearance Barbra flew back to Hollywood.

29

Funny Girl was released and the reviewers were ecstatic. A **Newsweek** critic called Streisand's performance, "the most accomplished, original, and enjoyable musical comedy performance ever put on film." Barbra was nominated for an Oscar but her competition was tough. In February of 1969, on Academy Award night, a tie was announced for best actress. Katherine Hepburn and Barbra Streisand were the winners. Barbra picked up her Oscar and said, "Hello Gorgeous!" — which was also the first line she spoke in the movie. The audience cheered.

After the success of **Funny Girl** it was hard to figure out what Streisand could or should do next. She was signed for the leading roles in two more musicals: **Hello Dolly**, and **On A Clear Day You Can See Forever**. **Hello Dolly** was panned by the critics, but Barbra still got good notices.

During 1969, after **Dolly** opened, Barbra and Elliot announced they were beginning an "amicable separation." Barbra told a reporter, "We've separated to save our marriage, not destroy it." Part of the problem was, as it often is in show business marriages, that Elliot and Barbra were both hungry for stardom, but Barbra's fame and fortune arrived before Elliot's. Elliot became a big movie star only after they were divorced.

During her latest interview, when asked if she is still close to Elliot, Barbra said, "Yes." She let it be known that they are close and that she does not want to discuss it.

Barbra's career moved forward with the film, **On A Clear Day You Can See Forever**. She got on well with her co-stars and with her director, Vincent Minnelli, and her personal reviews were the best of her career. After completing the movie, Barbra was asked what kind of an actress she thought she was and where she thought her strengths lay. She replied thoughtfully, "I guess my best attribute is my instinct. It just . . . it hurts me if I hear a wrong line reading or something. . . .It's like music. I mean, acting is even like music. Because I believe in rhythm, you know? Everything is so dominated by our heart-beats, by our pulses, when one goes against certain rhythms it's jarring, it's unnatural, unless we use the dissonance. I'm not articulate and I'm not eloquent. . . . It sounds just awful. I mean I hear it! But the point is I read a script and I just hear and I see what the people are doing and I'll have an idea right off the bat, and it's always my first instinct that I trust. I'm also very lazy so I don't delve much further." Besides instinct there is one other basic thing Streisand knows is important in order to be a good actress: confidence. "Anything carries when you have conviction," she says, "one little shred of doubt, though, and you've lost them all, you know?"

After three big musical movies Barbra decided it was time for a change. She signed to do a non-musical comedy called **The Owl and The Pussycat**. The comic teamwork between Barbra Streisand and George Segal and the excellent direction of Herbert Ross made **The Owl and The Pussycat** one of the most successful films of 1970.

After completing four films in three years Barbra took a vacation. In an interview in **Life** magazine, she said, "I look forward to working less and simplifying my life, to fulfilling some of my potential as an individual and as a woman. My little girl fantasy of being a recording star, a theater star, a concert star, and a movie star is impossible to maintain; each of them suffers. There is so much to learn; so much to do. What I'd like is more time . . . ."

Barbra also said, "I am terribly lazy. But maybe that's because I'm afraid if I worked harder, I wouldn't accomplish any more. . . . That's why I love being in the movies. I'm performing all over the world — while I'm sitting home taking a bath. I love the movies — life is so tentative and short that I want something to remain as proof that I existed."

During her year's rest Barbra worked in politics for Eugene McCarthy and Bella Abzug. She took over the chairmanship of the National

Association for Retarded Children and has served as Chairwoman for many years.

After a year away from film making, Streisand was ready to get back to work. She appeared in **What's Up Doc?**, directed by Peter Bogdanovich and starring Barbra and Ryan O'Neal. This movie, although the reviews were lukewarm, was a huge box-office success.

She then made a movie called **Up The Sandbox**, which told the story of a housewife who imagines herself into different, exciting situations, in order to relieve the boredom of her everyday life. Streisand worked hard to keep on good terms with the press and gave several interviews during the filming of this movie because, she said, "I care about **Sandbox**. I think it is a provocative film and I want to help it." Barbra also let it be known that there were similarities between her and the film character she portrayed. As she said, "There is a part of me that longs to stay home and be with my child . . . but there is another part of me that needs a form of expression other than bearing children. . . ."

The movie opened in New York to decidedly mixed reviews. The critics seemed either to love it or hate it, but most of Streisand's personal notices were, as usual, excellent. This movie was a breakthrough for Barbra because for the first time she portrayed a woman who was an ordinary human being with ordinary problems.

From this role Streisand went on to make the hugely successful film, **The Way We Were**, with Robert Redford. (Barbra's recording of the title song reached number one in the Charts.) Redford enjoyed working with her and said, "I liked her and we got along very well. I found her very talented, intelligent, insecure, and untrusting. Untrusting because she's been told too many lies; she's been hustled, misled, used, and jounced by too many hangers-on and hucksters."

Redford's is one of the strongest statements ever made in defense of Barbra. He reveals through his words the other side of Barbra that **she** says is there but that she rarely shows. Her vulnerability, her insecurity, though endearing to her friends, are rarely shown to anyone else. The bright and brashy side of Streisand is all she,

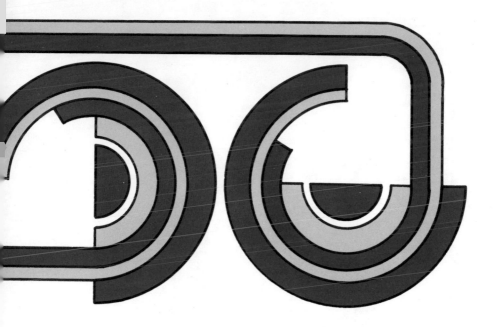

until recently, had shown of herself.

Barbra's last movie before **Funny Lady** was called **For Pete's Sake**. Once again, the movie received mixed reviews but Barbra got good notices. Then, for the first time in twelve years, Barbra seemed to disappear from the public eye. She had begun a new romance with a Hollywood hairdresser named Jon Peters. She was involved in the planning of **Funny Lady** as the sequel to **Funny Girl**, but there was no mention of her in any magazine or any T.V. program. During these years Streisand fans kept buying her record albums. Occasionally there were nasty comments about her and Jon in Gossip Columns, but Streisand seemed to have remained firm on her plan to stop giving interviews.

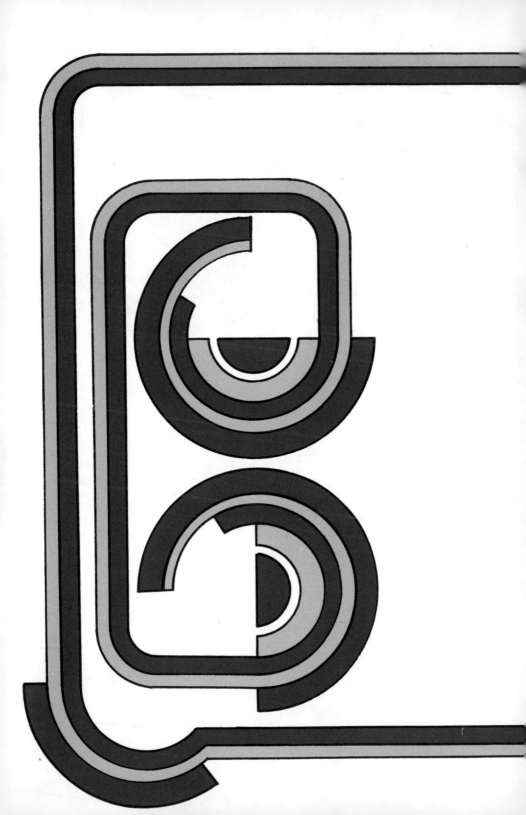

today

Barbra's face, covered with a veil, was on the cover of McCall's magazine in April, 1975. The subtitle under her name is "A superstar's struggle to become a woman." Two years had passed since Streisand permitted a written interview to be published. Suddenly, because she had completed **Funny Lady**, she consented to magazine and television interviews.

Barbra found her role in **Funny Lady** a challenge because she aged from a thirty-year-old woman to a fifty year old. Barbra felt that she got into the character of Fanny Brice and that she wasn't trying to be liked in this film the way she did in **Funny Girl**. It was a thrill for her to complete her interpretation of the character who gave her the biggest start in show business that any young star ever had.

During the **Today Show** interview early in 1975, Streisand seemed ready to talk about the movie or about her life. She appeared "natural." Her hair was straight and long and she had very little makeup on; or perhaps she had lots of make-up on but it was **natural** make-up, not make-up designed to disguise a face or a person. She was dressed in slacks and a sweater, looking casual.

Her usual flippant manner with an interviewer was gone. She talked easily, naturally, taking pains to be understood. She wanted to make clear to listeners and readers who she was and what she wants out of life. Comments like these were laced through the entire talk: "This is the most lucid time of my life . . . I see myself more clearly . . . I see what it is to be myself . . . I am learning the art of living."

When Barbara Walters asked her if it was fun being a superstar, Streisand replied, "You make it seem like it's fun. Sure . . . no . . . I'm a person. I feel very full of what I want out of my life. I've never been into enjoying my life . . . I want to make my life joyful. . . ."

This is a surer, more at ease, more self-confident Barbra. Recent interviews show that she doesn't go for the easy one line joke; she doesn't mock herself as she used to. She is paying attention now to who she is. Streisand once said, "The only true happiness I know is the happiness you can get from a soft baked potato with a nice hard shell." Now when she is asked the same question she replies, "The only true happiness is the true happiness I have with my family, with Jon."

Jon Peters is the man she's in love with now. She talks about Jon and about how they are alike and share many of the same dreams and plans, and she makes a revealing comment, saying, "In the past, when I didn't like myself, I was attracted to people unlike me." Now, apparently, she is not afraid of liking people like herself.

For the past few years Barbra has been finding out who she is. She has spent time with her son, with Jon, with friends, and with herself. Even Barbra has been confused about who she really is. The poses and masks she's adopted through the years have hidden her from herself.

In interviews, Barbra tells of her need to change and grow. She mentions how she used to feel out-of-touch with herself and she says, "I got tired of the same destructive patterns; I was putting up defensive walls; relationships were difficult for me. I was so full of fantasy about other people that I turned off anyone who wasn't perfect. What I didn't realize then was how hard it is to accept imperfection in others until you can accept it in yourself. And I got so tired of my craziness, and when you're that tired of something, you change. Anyone can change anything. I believe in the will. I always have . . . I decided that I wanted to be happy, that I wanted to be healthy. I was tired of the pain . . . I guess it was a matter of wanting to grow, wanting to survive."

So many things seem to have changed for Barbra Streisand, superstar. She shares, easily now, stories about herself and her son. Jason, she explains, goes to a public school and they go together to public beaches. She says that since no

one expects famous people to go to public beaches, anyone who sees them just says, "Oh, well, it can't be her." She thinks that providing a normal home for Jason will be good for him. Barbra feels that it is more realistic if he's with ordinary kids and if he goes with his mother to ordinary places.

Barbra seems more willing now to reveal her thoughts about her personal life. She doesn't use her humor as a weapon to keep people away. She seems to love her son and be relaxed with him. As she says, "I'm really beginning to enjoy my son. He's got a great sense of humor and he's at such a terrific age. I love watching him learn to read and write. Jon is really great with him too . . . he teaches him how not to be afraid. I wish I'd had someone to teach me that when I was Jason's age."

Such a straightforward statement reveals the person Barbra's been hiding for a few years. She admits freely that the working side of her grew up fast because it had to. "There wasn't time for everything. Something had to go and its was myself that went." Barbra is right. She was in plays at fourteen, out of her home at sixteen, and a superstar at twenty. She became a personality who was studied and examined by the public but she never had the time to examine or study herself. Now that she's taken the time she's happier and more open, not just with interview-

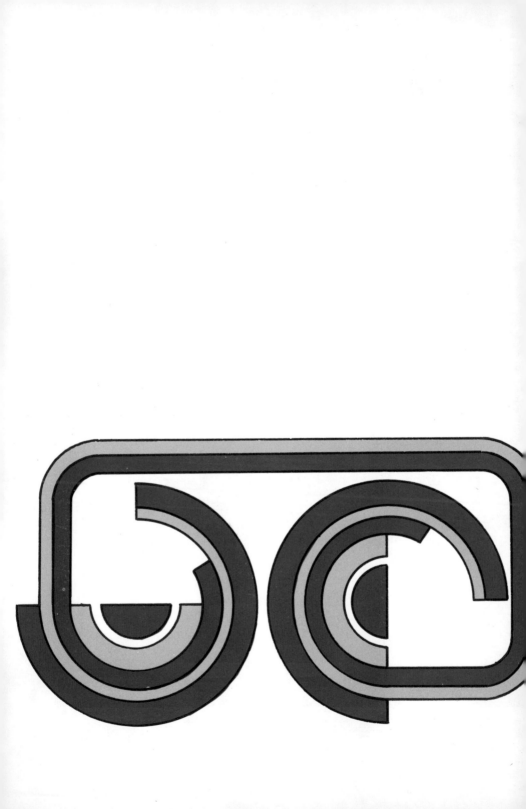

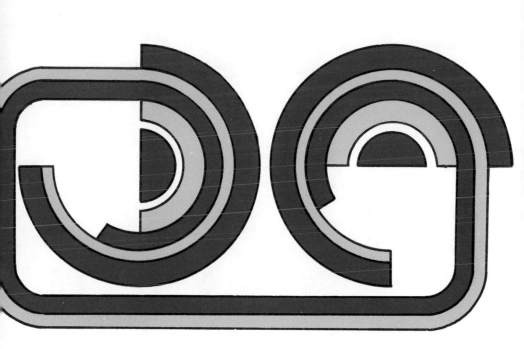

ers, but with her family and friends and with herself.

Barbra understands now that people view her in different ways. She knows some call her exotic and others say she's plain; some love her and some hate her. She seems comfortable with this awareness. She knows now that everything she does or says is risky because her statements and decisions can be misinterpreted. She says, "I've always taken risks in my career. I'm not going to do just what I'm expected to do. It's no fun for me. I'm not afraid of failure."

It seems that finally all the masks, all the disguises are gone. Barbra Streisand, superstar, is seen, at last, as a person. She likes herself now and perhaps that is the reason she's ready to let

45

herself be seen again. She has worked hard finding out who she is and what she wants; the same way she worked hard to make it out of Brooklyn and into show business.

Streisand is determined still, but finally, after years of work, she is taking time to relax and discover what her life is all about. A few years ago in an interview she said, "Who am I anyway? I'm waiting in a lobby and somebody over there smiles at me. What the hell is that stranger smiling at me for? Then I go, Oh, yeah. I guess I'm what's-her-name."

The difference today is that Barbra knows she's "what's-her-name," famous star, but she knows who Barbara Joan Streisand, the person is, too.